Cranes

by Charles Lennie

ABDO
CONSTRUCTION MACHINES
Kids

www.abdopublishing.com

Published by Abdo Kids, a division of ABDO, P.O. Box 398166, Minneapolis, Minnesota 55439.

Copyright © 2015 by Abdo Consulting Group, Inc. International copyrights reserved in all countries. No part of this book may be reproduced in any form without written permission from the publisher.

Printed in the United States of America, North Mankato, Minnesota.

052014

092014

 THIS BOOK CONTAINS RECYCLED MATERIALS

Photo Credits: Shutterstock, Thinkstock

Production Contributors: Teddy Borth, Jennie Forsberg, Grace Hansen

Design Contributors: Candice Keimig, Laura Rask, Dorothy Toth

Library of Congress Control Number: 2013952540

Cataloging-in-Publication Data

Lennie, Charles.

 Cranes / Charles Lennie.

   p. cm. -- (Construction machines)

ISBN 978-1-62970-017-5 (lib. bdg.)

Includes bibliographical references and index.

1. Cranes, derrick, etc.--Juvenile literature. 2. Construction equipment--Juvenile literature.   I. Title.

621.8--dc23

                    2013952540

Table of Contents

Cranes

Cranes mainly lift and move heavy objects. They help move **materials** at construction sites.

4

Crane Parts

Most cranes have the same main parts. The **operator** sits in the **cab**. A weight helps balance the crane.

cab

weight

7

The **boom** and **jib** act like long arms. They reach and move things.

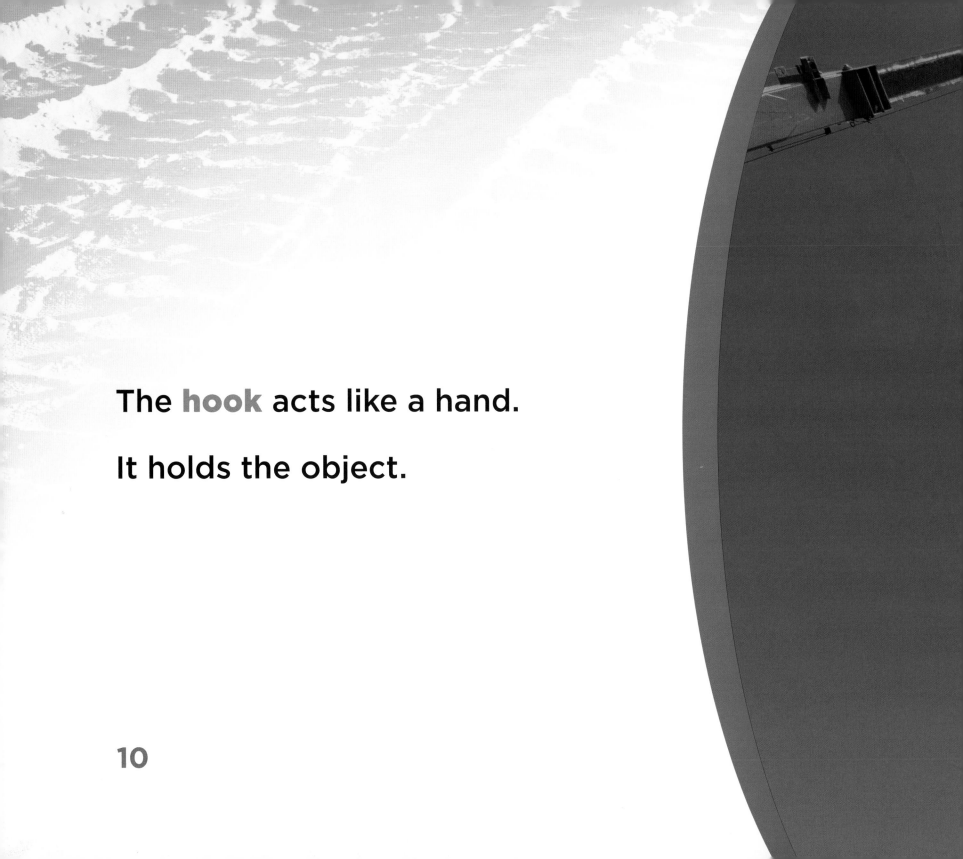

The **hook** acts like a hand.

It holds the object.

10

11

Some cranes move on **tracks**.

Other cranes move on wheels.

Different Kinds

Cranes come in many sizes. Small cranes work inside of workshops.

14

15

Big cranes help

build tall buildings.

17

Some cranes are **mounted** on trucks. Others do not move at all.

18

19

There are floating cranes.

They are used to build oil rigs.

More Facts

- The ancient Grecians and Romans were the first to use cranes. They were made from wood, ropes, and pulleys.

- The first cranes used manpower and animal power to do the lifting.

- Workers need to be sure that the crane is sitting on hard, even ground. Otherwise, the crane could tip over while it is lifting very heavy objects.

Glossary

boom – a long beam that holds the hook. The boom lifts and guides the hook.

cab – where the operator sits to control the machine.

hook – the hook holds the load. The hook is attached to a line that runs up the boom and jib.

jib – sometimes cranes have a jib attached to the boom. It extends to allow for the crane to reach farther.

material – anything used for construction, or making something else.

mount – to set or place on top of.

oil rig – a rig used for drilling oil or gas.

operator – the person controlling the machine.

track – continuous metal band around the wheels of a heavy vehicle.

Index

abdokids.com

Use this code to log on to abdokids.com and access crafts, games, videos and more!

Abdo Kids Code:
CCK0175